I0811038

DEAR BEAST

CATHERINE PIERCE

saturnalia | BOOKS

Distributed by Independent Publishers Group
Chicago

Saturnalia Books
2816 North Kent Rd.
Broomall, PA 19008
info@saturnaliabooks.com

ISBN: 978-1-947817-92-0 (print), 78-1-947817-93-7 (ebook)
Library of Congress Control Number: 2025947313

Book and Cover design by Robin Vuchnich

Distributed by:
Independent Publishing Group
814 N. Franklin St.
Chicago, IL 60610
800-888-4741

CONTENTS

for Mike

I'VE KNOWN YOU ALL MY LIFE

Animal inside me. No phylum for you,
no class. You are rough fur, satin scales,
plastic, lakewater, steel. Wings and candy wrappers.
Seaweed and hooves. You lunge. Whimper.
Lunge. Poison teeth. Gentle tongue.
Slither into the darkness and find
what you will. Dwell in the damp cave.
Curl up hearthside. Carry the spider. Devour
the bacon. Berries, berries, berries.
Howl. Caw. Crawl. The sun is hot and you leap
into waves. The sun is hot and you pant.
You are lazy for days. You won't stop running.
Reason can't rope your long neck. Dear beast.
Dearest beast. You let me get close.
You almost let me touch you.

THE WHENWOLF

The whenwolf is worried about
its dentist appointment. Its flu shot.
Its colonoscopy. It knows the cat
will die. It knows about the glaciers.
The whenwolf knows the sun
will expand and disintegrate the earth.
It also knows it will be long dead
by then, and isn't sure which bit
of knowledge is worse. The whenwolf
spends a lot of time reading
about extinction events. It knows
the gloomy tube-nosed bat was last seen
in 1962 but refuses to give up hope.
It wonders if its eyes are failing.
It wonders if its cough should be
checked out. It wonders if the thinning
backyard canopy is due to winter or
emerald ash borers. At night,
the whenwolf falls asleep thinking *not yet,*
please, not yet. It dreams its heart
as a small hourglass, blue sand falling
through the elegant neck until
the upper globe is almost, almost empty,
and then turning, just barely
in time, and starting again.

URGENCY

Something is happening in the woods behind the house.
Thousands of small black birds—maybe grackles,
you think—are congregating, loud as a cathedral
of swing sets. They're flying out from, then back into
the turning trees. They are saying something urgent

to each other. Today is the first frost, and maybe
it has to do with that and maybe not, you'll never know.
Every day in the woods: answered song or sudden hot mouth,
satisfied hunger or the moldering stage. In yellow elm
or chanterelle rot. In hollow log or sedge. Every day

you make your coffee, open the blinds, gird yourself
for the rigamarole of highway and committee. Every day,
jacket, phone, keys, the door locked behind you.
Meanwhile something is happening in the woods,
maybe the most important thing that's ever happened.

IF/WHEN

The poem I planned to write
was about last week's hurricane,

about how I live in Mississippi,
not so far from the storm's rages,

and how even still we felt
nothing here, nothing at all.

That was going to be the ending,
because I wanted to make a point

about how easy it is to ignore
disaster when it's not churning

directly over your town, and I was hoping
a reader might then extrapolate

a larger point about disturbance
and proximity, like how politicians

are always saying they used to oppose X
until some terrible Y happened

to their daughters, and it seems
to me we're requiring an awful lot

from daughters these days. Sons, too.
This week a message from my kids'

school district included the phrase *if/when*
a lockdown is ever necessary. The reason

I'm writing this poem instead
of the one I'd planned is that I keep

thinking about that email and also
now the hurricane was a week ago

and there's a new disturbance
forming near the Bahamas. And

last night Sioux Falls was tornado-
shredded and in Sterling, Colorado,

egg-size hail pummeled windshields,
and I guess what I'm saying is, why bother

with a poem about one hurricane,
one email? There will be more,

and there will be more,
and there will be more until

there is nothing left. The thing
about the poem I was going to write

is that it would have been a lie.
That nonsense about how we don't

feel it here. We feel it everywhere,
don't we? Dear daughter, dear son,

dear someone's something, we're well
past the *if* and into the *when.*

Talk about proximity—
some days I wear the world

like a skin. I am tired of waiting
for extrapolation. Let us all

be disturbances now.

WHAT I WANT TO BELIEVE ABOUT THE VIREOS

> "I have no idea why vireos are doing so well," Dr. Rosenberg said. "I'd love to do a study of vireos and discover what their secret is."
>
> —*The New York Times*, "An Ecological 'Crisis' as 2.9 Billion Birds Vanish"

The vireos are plotting.
They are everywhere and various

and all with names
like Shakespearean villains

disguised as Shakespearean clowns.
Black-whiskered.

Plumbeous. Slaty-capped
shrike. Their songs drop

from the canopy like candied
needles, and everyone smiles. Sweet

birds. They've been above us
for centuries, watching. See

their eyes: small bright
pebbles that betray

nothing. They know
patience. See them tableau'd

on the oak branch
for minutes before diving

for the fat black beetle.
They know how green works,

how it muscles back, always,
once the pillars and poisons

are gone. They're playing
the long game. *Weary,*

weary, weary, trills the scrub
greenlet. It'll all be theirs

again—rain forests, mangroves,
the great deciduous rustle.

The breeze and moss.
The loam and sunrise.

The vireos will be here
at the end and at the next

beginning. The red-eyed
vireo's call will sound then

like it does now, like
it's constantly asking

and answering
its own questions.

What did they do?
They did.

What did they know?
They knew.

WHAT DO YOU MAKE OF THAT?

I make of it a small ship
sinking. A red-gleam apple,

underside soft brown,
maggoted. I make of it poison

sumac. The thick stillness
that precedes a tin roof torn off.

I make of it last ocean swim,
last orangest tulip, last Malbec

unfettered by last. I make of it
a loom on which I daily weave

my own undoing, the wefts
what ifs, the warps the *when*.

I make of it a sharp pine needle
at my back, urging me forward.

I make of it, sometimes,
propulsion, Lake Lucerne

in June, the tickets booked.
I make of it *yes*. I make of it *maybe*

never again, so. I make of it *but now*.
I make of it the corn maze

in October, the sad dry stalks
but my god that sky

behind them. And I make of it
how I only love that sky more—

hot blue, so bright it stings—
the further in I go.

AT 42, I CONSIDER BECOMING A ZOOKEEPER

It comes to me as I'm tweezing my eyebrows,
just after I've washed my face with the same

mentholated soap I've used since I was fifteen.
These nightly ablutions. It's not too late.

Likely not the lions, with their meat-red maws.
Not the polar bears, upright towering to two of me,

their loom-and-menace I've seen museum-taxidermied
too many times. But the lynx, the ibis,

the blue-eyed black lemur. The giraffes with their long
purple tongues. I could tend the capybara.

I could tend the gibbon. It's not too late,
refrain I've been singing all my life, beloved chorus.

I'll be singing it until it is, and maybe after. The fossa
with her impossible round ears. The zebras. The otters.

I imagine the meerkats surrounding me as I enter
their pseudo-savanna with a silver bucket. I place

mealworms and apples gently into their dishes.
Their soft eyes watch. I am an absolute fucking hero.

BURROWING CRAYFISH (AN ODE)

You're gilled but till the soil
like any earth-snug vertebrate.
You never read the manual.
Your armor slick and essential,
your antennae, your pincers—
you off-put glibly, confound
propriety. Late spring,
and your mud chimneys
turret up from storm-marshed
backyards. No one invited you.
You don't care. You feast
on what's desiccated or deliquesced.
Detritivore, you know
there's no shame in a name.
Someone is calling you mudbug,
someone is calling you crawdad,
someone is calling you nightmare-in-the-yard,
and you don't give a good goddamn.
Build your towers high, little beast.
Flummox the mowers, taunt dogs,
turn stomachs. Take what you want,
your rotting leaves, your worms.
Dig deep for the water. Then
glisten to the surface again,
vulgarly, audaciously alive.

SHOOTING GALLERY, OR WHAT I DON'T SAY WHEN I WRITE TO MY SENATORS AGAIN ABOUT GUN SAFETY

I was ten and it was perfect: the cool
metal of the trigger against my index finger,

the nub of the sight, the stock solid
against my skinny shoulder. I slid

my quarter into the slot and for two minutes
an entire saloon was mine to make dance.

The barrel, lid tipping to reveal a raccoon.
The mounted moosehead suddenly alive.

The snake would rattle, the vulture caw,
and if I was lucky and lined up just right,

I could make the man hunched over the piano
play a quick, desperate rag. It hurt

just enough, squeezing the metal hard
to make the pop, to make the tin cans

jump, the spigot run water. It was like magic
to me, how I pulled the trigger here

and fifteen feet away the red-and-white target
flipped down and the cuckoo burst

from the clock. What sent the message?
What made the machinery listen? It was

a kind of miracle: with a quarter and my hand,
I caused everything to happen. I was small,

but the world moved for me.

CHANGE

Some nights I wish my rage could lupinize me,
my jaw stretched and menacing,
my teeth so fierce I'd no longer care
about the small and tedious details of how
humans try or don't to keep one another
alive. I could run on wrath,
eyes incandescent and unignorable.
I could rip apart any soft, thoughtless thing.
I am so tired of manners. I've been
manacled too long to caution. This country
is a terrible animal, snuffling foolishly
through gardens, uprooting anything
the farmers have carefully sown. Soon
we'll have no crops to make it through winter.
Watch me changing. It hurts,
but now there is no way back—
I am elongating, I am sprouting hackles
and claws. I see this beast stand upright,
taller than the horses. I see this beast
throw back its head. We howl and howl.
The animal of this country watches,
then turns back to the sweet, tender roots.

THE WHYWOLF

The whywolf has questions about flower stamens.
The whywolf doesn't get why lightbulbs work,
not the electricity part but the mechanism itself.
The whywolf's search history is full of questions
like "Why do airplanes crash" and "Why do
people get divorced" and "Why cancer" and
"Why wasps." The whywolf wants to be able
to fix everything, if we're being honest. It wants
to prepare for any terrible maybe or eventuality
so as to most efficiently stem or stopper or instantly
obliterate it. The whywolf is pretty sure that enough
understanding will render the wild world safe.
That nightmare unknowns are just dark rooms
and knowledge is a floodlight. It has to be this way,
thinks the whywolf. It has to. Because.

OH, TODAY WAS ACTUALLY THE LONGEST DAY OF THE YEAR

I said to my husband. We'd thought it was the next day
but we were wrong. The virus was a few months old.
In Tulsa the president railed to a half-empty arena. No one
wore masks, because they were brave and understood
the manipulative nature of science. On Twitter

a friend had posted Daisy Buchanan's quote—
do you always watch for the longest day of the year and then
miss it? I always watch for the longest day in the year and then miss it—
and I didn't even give it a cursory heart, though
I've always loved that line, its repetition, how clearly

it conveys Daisy's nervousness, her false bravado,
how she's trying to convince herself of who she is.
Today was actually the longest day of the year, I said
to my husband, and he said, *Oh, was it?* and then,
But tomorrow's the first day of summer, right? and I said

I don't know and then thought *I don't care*, and
that's quite a thing because if I know anything
about myself it's that I most definitely care
about the first day of summer. I care about the solstice,
I care about the word *solstice*, I care about light,

more light, about how those were Goethe's
last words and I tried for years to write a poem
about them but never could because those words
were the poem, I care about the evening sky in late June
all orange and blazing and the roaring absolute

opposite of a half-empty arena, I care about twilight
mosquitos and their quaint diseases, I care
about care, I care about awful Daisy Buchanan
and her gin and her daughter and the fried chicken
she ate with Tom the same night she tore a woman's

breast from her body with an absurd yellow Rolls Royce,
I care about the longest day of the year, I do, I do,
but in that year every day was the longest day
and somehow still there was no more light, just a
half-haze that fogged cars and sun and justice

and I thought about the beaches rippling with bright
bathing suits and sunblock sheen, and I thought about
the smiling parents who, at their son's 5th birthday party
the winter before the world closed, balloons and homemade
favors and gorgeous fondant-wrapped cake, told me

they weren't political, and I thought of Daisy
wishing her daughter to be a beautiful fool
and then saying to Nick, so earnest or duplicitous,
You see I think everything's terrible anyhow, as if
she could live in the world while tossing it away.

SOME THINGS ARE NOT HYPOTHETICAL

Like, for instance, cattails. Or my necklace
strung with silver cattails. Or N95 masks.
Or the dying we will all most certainly,
unavoidably, someday do. I like
the concreteness of concrete. I like
the absolute thereness of the Gravitron.
I appreciate how, when I drive past
a highway field where a skunk recently
sprayed, suddenly my entire car
is skunk. I like the parts of the world
you can count on. So many mornings
I have trouble getting out of bed—
my mind on calls that could
turn sour, my thumb quick-flicking
through the day's bad-but-might-
get-worse news. I do better when
I spring up with my alarm—
the shower is not hypothetical.
The plastic razor. The coconut shampoo.
Hypothetical is if I slip. Hypothetical
is if this mole looks different. Hypothetical
is what the day holds once I drop
the kids at school, once I pull back
onto the highway. The very quiet student
and his backpack. The cop car followed
by speeding ambulance. It's the long, trembling
weekend after the biopsy. A loud bang.
A rustling. Hypothetical is what happens

after I walk into my classroom wearing
an N95 and my necklace of cattails,
each frozen in the illusion of bending,
cast forever in the moment
before the moment that follows.

WORDS FAIL

I smooth *bramble* into my skin,
bathe in *dragonfruit*. Swallow *hyacinth*
like a fast-acting capsule. *O'erfraught,*
says Malcolm to MacDuff and I
tuck it behind my ear. *Lionlimb,*
writes Hopkins, and it opens
into a crystalline umbrella.
I ribbon my hair with *gild*
and *gloss* and *sorrel*. *Cellophane*
is a chandelier. *Burnish*, a soft
black cat. *Virus* is a poorly-made
rucksack, one that sits low and wide
and never fits in the overhead.
Climate is a tight synthetic shoe.
Precautions and *increase,* a pair
of nickel-plated studs whose posts
itch and vex my ears. *Thoughts and prayers*
and everywhere: hives. To soothe,
I salve with *Ferris wheel*. I take a dram
of *alluvial*, and then of *dram*. It helps,
but I've got *these days* still taut
around my wrist, bracelet of gilded
brambles I can't unclasp.

PROBABLY IT WILL BE SUMMER AGAIN

(March 2021)

Probably it will be summer again
one of these days, and if it is I'll swim,
bobbing up and down over *probably*,
it will be summer and hello, my god I'll say hello
to people who don't live in my house,
it will be summer and my eyes reluctant after a full day
of refracted ocean light and dolphin-squint, or maybe
library and carousel and everyone's bright
skirts, bright sunglasses, bright burns and canvas bags,
I'll rejoin the perpetual chorus of *We should*,
perpetual chorus of *Let's*, my god my best friend's baby
who's talking now, my god the bay is still there
and I promise I will be a fool for humans and all
wild proclivities, I will gently turn horseshoe crabs
right-side-up, I will not tell myself *Maybe a meteor*
or *Maybe a phone call* or *Maybe a sudden shift*
in atmosphere, I will remind myself of mouths
moving in ways that are summer and of my skin
casual next to someone else's skin and the soft
salt smell and haunted house shrieks, and *Probably*
I will say, *Probably* I will make myself say, and I will say it
and I will say it until it is who and where,
it is who and where we are.

POEM NOT INTENDED TO STAND IN CONTRAST TO ANYTHING FOR ONCE

This is an earnest ode to the yellow leaves
rattling like tambourines against the November sky.
To the song of my dog's collar jangling as she high-steps

into the crisp morning. What a sun. What a pine.
What a cardinal. This is a love poem to each person
crowded around The Starry Night at the MoMA,

phones held high, and to all of the photos mainly
of phones held high. This is not a poem about how once
we could crowd around The Starry Night at the MoMA

and then we couldn't. This is not a poem about once,
although yes once, and I have other poems about that.
But not this one. This is a poem about

the water tower I can see from my kitchen window,
how it picks up morning light, sunset light, twilight
and gleams it back to our town like a modest, dutiful beacon.

This is a poem for my children still sleeping at 7:30
on a Saturday morning. This is a poem for dusky purple
nail polish. For the word *bourguignon*. For aspen.

For Aspen. For fiddler crabs. I keep going back
to those leaves. Look, one morning I walked out
and the tree was green. The next week I walked out

and it was gold, like bright bright gold, unapologetic
and brazen. I didn't earn all that color. I just opened
the door and stepped outside. And it was there.

DOMESTIC BEAST

You snatch the wasp from the window.
Claw at the booted-in mud. Heft
carrots from the earth by their roots.

You are on high alert, always.
Sometimes you watch the mirror
like you don't trust the animal there.

Always, you're surrounded
by the body—the swept gray
of shed skin cells, the soft palm
held firm while you pluck the thorn.

You sterilize steel with fire.
Comb corners for the tracked-in days.

Sometimes you howl and birds scatter.
Sometimes you call and cats come.
Your voice is a forest's register;
it can never be wholly catalogued.

Each morning you rise before
the house is awake. The day
is not day yet, mist-cloaked
and gray. Your mind is a great horse
breathing steam into the still winter air.
It paws at the ground. It waits,
muscles twitching, for the sun.

YEAR IN REVIEW: 2020

I missed summer before it happened,
and then I missed it again. Daily my body
worried me, and I muttered *hush*.
My house buzzed with e-ghosts
of teachers, friends, river otters
from a zoo in Ohio. There was a puppy
livestream. Later, there was a puppy.
Hush, I told my body. I painted
my nails teal and lilac, o flimsy bravado.
I paced my street back and forth,
counted my steps, reversed direction
quickly when a boy on a bike veered near.
I stopped caring whose feelings I hurt.
I cared too much.
Orchid stamps!
Glossy pink postcards!
Each bulk order of filters
and alcohol wipes a sturdy wooden block
I placed on top of another,
my hands steady as a surgeon's.
I built the blocks into a perimeter but
inside it was the puppy,
was the summer,
was my body and the bodies
of everyone I loved and so
the blocks toppled with their heavy, predictable
clunk, again and again.
Still, I clicked.

I autofilled.
I anticipated
the delivery of sanitizer, the sleek black mail scale.
Hush, I said, *hush*. One night
I stayed up past midnight
finishing a 500-piece bird puzzle.
My god, the relief
when half a yellow wing
snapped right into place.

SURPRISE ME

I am tired of how predictable everyone is.
Same voices, same decibel levels, same words
tossed sloppily as meat to cartoon dogs.
Just once I'd like the comments to be filled

with recipes for excellent tiramisu or speculation
as to the whereabouts of Atlantis. Just once
I'd like the pundit known for jocular cruelty to break
into unironic song. Let all the aunts of disinformation

suddenly share Mayo Clinic infographics;
let the loudest school board member stay quiet
for just this one meeting. I want to walk down
to a river, any river, and watch the sun set over it,

gold and glittering. I want to sit on the bank
while behind me rises the city of my imagining,
the impossible city governed only by quiet
and the true, delicate flights of accurate birds.

SCREEN TIME

Turn off the screens and go outside,
I bark at my kids, caricature of *mother*,
while my own laptop is open again
to the map of new cases, the country
blotched purple and red, apoplectic.
I'm almost finished this round, my son says.
I'm so close to beating this boss, says my other son.
I don't answer; I'm busy refreshing
the page to see if anything's changed.
In their game where a big-eyed avatar
buys supplies from a mercenary raccoon,
day unfolds in real time.
The sky on the TV is the same
as the sky out the window, except
the TV-sky is mosquito-less, windless.
Sunset here, sunset on the coded island.
We watch the screen in awe
as behind us the real sky throws its color
against the sliding glass doors.
There is so much to marvel at,
and who's to say what's worthy of wonder?
We're all doing our best, aren't we?
We're here together. We'll take the dog
for a walk. We'll look at the redbuds.
We'll race each other through streets
hectic with flames and coins and sentient plants,
ignore each other for beasts or breaking news,
escape and then escape from the escape.

We'll live right here in the present future,
all our tenses scrambled, no idea where we are
or where we're going, navigating by
any lodestars that will load or shine.
I mean, look at the dog sniffing the crocus.
Look at the sword's glint, the arrow's arc.
Look at these skies. All of them.

THE WHOWOLF

Once the whowolf wore nothing
but large flannel shirts and torn jeans.

Once the whowolf wore nothing
but vintage prom gowns.

Once the whowolf ate only soy
hot dogs, only rare meat, only every

ice cream on the boardwalk shop's
100 Zany Flavors! menu.

Once the whowolf looked in the mirror
and said *hey baby*, said *buck up*, said *oh no*,

said *hell yes*. The whowolf was so many
wolves. The whowolf walked

beside itself and kept good company.
Don't worry, everyone said, *someday*

you'll figure out who you are. But
this is a happy story, because

the whowolf never did.

EARTH, SOMETIMES I TRY TO PLAY IT CASUAL,

like *Hey mercury, hey malachite, I'm busy today,*
can't stop to marvel, but always my blood is saying
O god you starsprung miracle. It's self-preservation,

letting myself believe laundry matters,
letting myself believe there's anything other than
egrets and oceans and vast moss carpets and

the finite heart of every single person I love.
Earth, you terrify me—you are fierce green
and honeysuckle, you are herds of wild ponies,

and you are leaving, always. Is it any wonder
some days I look at my laptop instead of out
the window? Every time I glance up

there you are, quaking me with your fern fronds
and silver frost. O you of the rhyolite mountains.
You of the dew-hung web. You are lemon quartz

and quicksand. Muskrats and starfish. How
could I be any way but staggered? O blue spruce,
O white fir, O green forever, you know

my nonchalance is a sham. It's so hard to admit
our real desires. Earth, what I want is to sit gentle
under your twilight purple, watch your bats

hunt and dive. What I want is to know about
endings and still love each wingbeat, each shade
of the boundless, darkening sky.

AT THE RETIREMENT HOME FOR THE LASTS

The last woman to eat shrimp cocktail in a transatlantic zeppelin
plays canasta with the last woman to have heard Bessie Smith

perform live. The last man born on a day when no one feared
nuclear bombs watches *Harvey* with the last woman

to use the phrase "the living end" unironically. Overhead,
the last Bachman's warbler flits tree to tree, its jeweled yellow

spangling first this green, then that. A man—the last
to have purchased a just-released copy of *Rebecca*—

touches the white tendrils of the last ghost orchid gently, as if
it might startle. The last red pencilfish flashes through

the ornamental pond, watched by the last woman to have danced
at the Stork Club, all those years and colors and songs ago.

No one visits this place; no one knows where it is.
Only the lasts, together in the last sunsoft afternoons,

last thick-blanket nights, last sweet air and water-quench days,
know where to find one another. When a new last arrives,

they're welcomed with love and grief and black-eyed susans—
all abundant, nowhere near vanishing.

POTENTIAL ENERGY

In September a man stole a plane
and threatened to crash into the Tupelo Wal-Mart,
and my first thought was *At least*
it's not a gun. A month earlier,
my oldest son had Covid. His brother
slid a note under his quarantine door
saying, "I hope you feel better."
In every moment there is so much potential
grief and potential tenderness waiting
to burst and sow itself, like the seed pods
of the pink impatiens I loved growing up.
Come August I was greedy for the coiled green
that sprang open under my lightest pinch
and erupted tiny black BBs of possible flowers.
On meet-the-teacher night I surveyed
the sixth-grade hallway and wished
it was down a less central wing so a gunman
would be more likely to kill someone else's
child first, and there is nothing all right
about that, there is nothing all right
about the way my jaw tightens every time
I hear yelling on the school playground
behind my house, the way I know
without clicking why a city name is trending,
the way, when my sister texted me
that her kids were on lockdown
because of a bear outside their school,
I thought, *At least it's just a bear*. At least
it's just a bear. The man in Tupelo

eventually landed the plane. While circling,
he'd posted a message to Facebook saying
he never actually wanted to hurt anyone,
and I thought about that *actually* all night.
He didn't actually hurt anyone in the end,
not if we measure hurt by wreckage and debris.
My oldest son lets the dog lick his face.
He asks for a new pair of basketball shoes. He says
what if a shooter comes to his school. I say,
That's very, very unlikely, sweetheart, my coiled heart
ready to spring, to sow its useless ammunition.

BULLET IS A GOOD NAME FOR A HORSE

> "But in the middle of the second verse, I got tired. I had a tune, and I didn't want to waste the tune; it was a nice little melody, so I just wrote a quick third verse, and I recorded that."
>
> —Bob Dylan on "John Wesley Harding," *Rolling Stone* (1969)

For years, I told myself it was all right to still love
the gun in old Westerns. Because
it's maybe six chambers, maybe a small magazine,
and maybe it kills a man, yes, and we write
a song about that, but it's one man,
or maybe a few, but not fifty-nine people in a dance club
or twenty-seven in an elementary school,
and everyone who dies is fiction, after all.
I told myself it was all right because of all the preparatory clicking,
the theatrics of spinning and drawing,
that built-in escape time. Because today
no headline is about the Winchester.
Because once I sang "John Wesley Harding" as a lullaby
to myself, sweet lilt of how he *traveled*
with a gun in every hand, and felt tall-booted,
fierce-spurred. I wanted to be horseback.
I wanted to be outlaw. I was young
and thought a song could be a talisman.
Like if I wore a raincoat of rifles-
in-verse, I could walk through a shoot-out unscathed.
Forgive me. I know a jamming six-round
pistol still killed some mother's son.

I know raincoats work best when made
of vinyl, or nylon, or gabardine—
unromantic fabric, dull as legislation.
Dylan added the "g" to John Wesley Hardin's name
by mistake, or maybe because he wanted
a better sound, one unfettered by facts.
He chose the name because
it fit the tempo he'd already written.
He had no idea, he told the interviewer,
what his song was about.

SAND CRAB (AN ADMISSION)

Each summer I plunge my hands deep into sand,
scrape knuckles against millennia of rock, dig until

I feel against my palm the wriggling that means
success. I don't shriek or flinch. I'm skilled

at the capture, the catch and cradle, then
in my palm the prize: pink-gray carapace,

eyestalks like tendrils, ten white legs frantic
for the dark. I am teaching my children

how to dig for treasure, how to let touch
be their underground guide. I am teaching them,

I tell myself, kindness, because each beach day,
a hundred times each beach day, I say

keep the bucket water cold and *be gentle*
and *it's probably time to let them go now.* Still,

I keep digging. I love how every kid in earshot
runs to share the jackpot of secret creatures. I love

my bravery, plunging my soft hand into
the unknown. I love the startle of unearthing

one, smooth and curved as a tumbled stone,
and finding at underbelly the orange iridescence,

a thousand eggs like tiny sugared beads.
I love, too, my generosity when I say

Let's let this one go, and gently lower the sand crab
to the surf. *Look*, I say as she scuttles away,

we made her happy. What I never say is
Go, so that my children can catch yours.

POEM BEGUN WHILE WATCHING MY SON'S GYMNASTICS CLASS

Coltish is how we describe the children
when they ricochet, all knees and chaos,
through our homes, mud everywhere,
walls scraped, and we smile ruefully, or
shoo them outside, or snap *What are you*
thinking? and hope the neighbors don't hear,
but until right now I have never considered
the animal itself, wild-limbed and pent
in tasteful two-story, never considered how
a coffee table or ceiling fan or towering
bookcase has no place in the windswept
prairie, never considered how strange
the kitchen's cool tile must feel
under hooves built for grasslands
golden and lawless.

EARTH DAY

I ordered ecofriendly lipstick and it came
boxed in a box and padded with bubble wrap.
Every time I use it, I remember I'm a fool.
My town stopped curbside recycling because
it wasn't cost-effective; now if you pay
for the service, you can drive
your beer cans to the processing center.
Not your bottles, though—no glass.
On bad days, I know it doesn't really matter,
my small pinwheel of human acts spinning
against the great corporate turbine.
I'm cynical about Earth Day, its logos
and aggressive green, the petitions by which
I try to absolve myself. Why bother
flattening the cornflakes box? Why not buy
the leaf blower, the plane ticket, the excellent
New York strip? We know exactly how
all of this will go. Even still, I'm breaking down
the damn boxes. Listen: on Earth Day
years ago, at a street festival in Missouri,
my friends adopted a puppy. Two weeks later
their living room was somber,
their house sharp with the everywhere
smell of bleach, the puppy quarantined
with parvo. We knew he would die. And he did,
but not then. He died fifteen years later,
in Brooklyn, having been loved well all his days,
having met and adored my friends' two children,

having spent summers on Lake Champlain
and winters curled under a wooden
butcher block table from which fell
the most flavorful and elaborate scraps.
What do we know of what we know?
Let us recognize we are fools, and keep going.

IN WHICH I IMAGINE UNKINDLY NAMED PLANTS AS MIDDLE SCHOOLERS

Dear cut-leaved toothwort,
your boning-knife leaves will spark
hissing; know it for jealousy.

Dear punctureweed,
someone will love you.

Dear leatherleaf, dear hog peanut,
ignore the others in their meadow,
the nodding ladies' tresses
with their simpering, the starry campion
all fringed and spotlit.

Dear hairy beardtongue,
bide your time.

Dear common fleabane,
root together and be mighty.

Dear mouse-ear chickweed,
I see your small petals, green velvet
underneath.

Dear climbing boneset,
don't despair. You are clever
and dexterous and the showy evening
primrose is a pavement-creeper.

Dear rattlesnake master,
wear your name like a holy mantle.

Dear crown vetch,
stay pink and uncowed.

Dear bastard toadflax,
let them call your hunger
parasitic. Get what you need
however you can. Know
you'll increase
with fire.

THE HORSE GIRLS

The horse girls were writing novels.
The horse girls were dreading flag football.

The horse girls were silent
the long bus ride home, hating the boys
with their sex words and sloppy mouths.

The horse girls were reading at recess.
Before bed, they brushed around braces,

or turned small keys that opened the roofs
of their mouths. The horse girls
were toothy and gangle-limbed.

Their hair, embarrassed. Their shirts, ruffled
with anger. By the slide, beauties

in Benetton blouses cantered
around them, hooting, and the horse girls
did not look for teachers. They set

their toothy teeth, practiced a proud
carriage. The horse girls were saving quarters.

They were sliding their hands down
silken fetlocks, lifting and picking
hooves clean, careful always

of the tender inner arrow. The horse girls
were acing pre-algebra, toting

their oboes. They were reading
Flowers in the Attic. They were climbing
into their mothers' Camrys,

smelling of manure and getaways.
At night they were rocking against

their own hands in their dark bedrooms,
guilty over everything, galloping
toward the years where they'd leap

each ditch and stream with ease, where
they'd nab the gold cup every time.

I WONDER IF THE GUY WHO CATCALLED ME IN THE BLOCKBUSTER PARKING LOT WHEN I WAS 15 EVER THINKS ABOUT THAT

When the Jeep revved up

what I saw was three or four or thirty guys
laughing   three or four or thirty heads of blond hair
mouths of white teeth   and
one of them yelled out something
about my ass or taking me for a ride I don't know

because it's been 30 years but what I do
remember is that I spun around and said *Fuck off*

middle finger raised like a flare gun

and it was not the first time
I'd felt the hot fizz of fury but it was
the first time I'd uncorked it   and I remember
how his face slackened and the mouths
said *ooooh* and the blond heads
drove away in the cartoon-yellow Jeep

and when I got back in the car
where my parents and sister had been waiting
while I returned the VHS tapes

my mother said *What's so funny* because
I couldn't stop laughing and I said
Nothing   which was true   nothing

was funny at all I was laughing
because as I'd let my rage rise
and buzz my tongue and spill forth

I'd known suddenly that I had
an endless supply that it could fuel me
forever if I let it

MIDLIFE BEAST

Why now, with your teeth still strong enough
to tear meat from bone, corn from cob,
now with your legs faster, more muscled
than they've ever been, now with back

and arms strong enough to carry a child,
firewood, all-the-groceries-in-one-trip,
why now do you look at the doe in the woods,
the fox sleeking through the yards

with the violet thread of envy sewn through
your gaze? The deer will fall soon to rifle, coyote,
ice blue winter. The fox will try to cross
the road and not reach the other side.

Your hands are nimble. Your appetite vast.
Your eyes are weaker now, yes, but when
you call up your voice from your open throat,
the air all around you trembles.

THE WHEREWOLF

The wherewolf has been trudging
a long time through plains and deserts.
Through suburbia and forests
and strip mall parking lots.
The wherewolf has been
to the Lake District. Dubai.
The Arctic Circle. Has been pelted
with hail and Coke cans. Has wrested
grubs from mossed trees, spent
entire weeks drinking nothing
but icicle melt. It's seen
the Northern lights and Carnivale,
watched monks slip silently
through heavy wooden doors.
The wherewolf doesn't know
how old it is, or when
it started traveling. It knows
somewhere is home, but no place
rings the bell that sings *here*.
Sometimes people approach
with outstretched hands, holding
meat or blackberries, fingers curved
gently in a way that says
I mean no harm, and the wherewolf
wants to stop, wants to sit
at the people's feet and feel
its great ears smoothed back,
wants to savor the heft and smoke

of the offered meat, wants to stop
even for a night, an hour, a minute,
but there's so much
to see and run from and save,
so many places full of silk and razors,
and the wherewolf is tired, so tired,
but can't stop walking
through wind and traffic,
through parade shouts and waterfalls,
all the time listening for the distant bell
that never rings.

ENGINE, OR WHAT I AM LEARNING FROM THE ANIMALS

August in Mississippi and everything is turning
atmosphere. My sunglasses fog. My hair clouds.
On the porch, the board game left out overnight

warps like heat waves rising. Everywhere, green—
crepe myrtles, kudzu, moss, vines, sapling-weeds
thick as thumbs. When I say wildness

thrives here, I mean I'm afraid to step outside
in the morning. I mean I'm afraid to walk
into my dark kitchen at night. So many lives

drinking this wet air, growing longer, leggier
in the heat. Lizard in the linen closet, cockroach
flickering under bedroom door. Centipede

brazen on the porch swing, too thick to smash.
Orbweavers thread every acreage of this state—
golden, orchard, starbelly. *Is it even Mississippi,*

asked a friend, *if you don't get a spider or four*
in the face every time you go out? But lately
I'm telling myself to go out anyway, to walk

down the dark hall barefoot. Lately I'm trying
to save my fear for what matters. Hear its engine
inside me, how it revs my heart. What laziness

to waste its heat on small beasts when
there's so much to melt down: deliberate cruelty,
AR-15s, the phrase *the benefit of your views*.

Dear animals, teach me. You know how
to turn fear to fuel. I've seen you rebuild
the wrecked web thread by thread, watched you

scurry behind the baseboard with two legs
gone. Sometimes the engine inside me
stalls out—so many news alerts, the flags

full time at half-mast—but you keep going, keep
going. Just yesterday a lizard darted out
from under my bed. Too slow, I caught

only its tail with a glass. The tail twitched
for a few minutes, but the lizard, busy
with the work of survival, never looked back.

BREAK

Today is wind and the screams of chase
from the playground behind my house.
You'll see I couldn't bear to break
the line on "screams." You'll see
I chose to break the line on "break."
There I go again. Sometimes I engage
in magical thinking, as if by keeping
"screams" and "of chase" together
I remove all threat of anything terrible
that might otherwise be implied.
Now the recess monitor hollers through
her bullhorn, and while I wish she wouldn't
yell, I also know that whatever
she's getting paid isn't enough
to be walking every day into a box
of virus and bureaucracy's
crisscrossing lasers. Last week
I got the results of a biopsy:
negative, all normal. I broke after
the colon right there to build a little
suspense, which I allowed
because I have the results in hand,
can access the patient portal any time,
the words clear and downloadable.
But before the message came
I was heart-racing, humming
like an electric bee, no lunch, thanks,
no coffee. The biopsy was only

precautionary—*I'd be shocked*,
said my doctor—but by Day 12
my reserves of reason had run dry.
What I'm saying is, it takes a lot
of work to control everything.
To make sure a poem doesn't manifest
nightmare. To keep a teeming playground
from turning into a massacre.
To harness the bucking beast of fear,
slip in the bit and ride it steady
through your life without it bolting
wild into the vast fields around you.
With horses they call it breaking.

MY FATHER TAKES ME TO SEE THE 32-FOOT-TALL STAINLESS STEEL MADONNA SCULPTURE IN DOWNTOWN WILMINGTON DE

(Our Lady of Peace, sculpture by Charles C. Parks)

I was five when we drove into the city,
into the plaza with its tall silver buildings, parked
and walked right up to her, tilting our heads back
to take her in. Her great gleaming countenance.
Her elegant hands. I did not understand how this
was the woman with the fingerless lace gloves
and alarmingly beautiful lipstick, but my father said
it was Madonna so I knew it was, and I knew
she was special because my father said she was only
here for a little while, would soon be driven across
the country to a state I'd never seen and so this
was our chance to look at her, our only chance,
and so I gazed up, confused but reverent, adrift
for the first time in the great gray chasm that opens up
behind everything impermanent, which is everything.

ABECEDARIAN FOR THE POWER OUTAGE

Absolute, the sudden silence—the fan stops
buzzing, the refrigerator hushes. No,
child, the nightlight can't turn on. The nervous
dog curls herself like a comma against any soft thing.
Everything un-house—crickets, wind rustle,
full white moon—is amplified. Everything else: vanished.
Goodbye, breaking and broken news; farewell, accomplishing. Dear
husband, shall we fool around? Dear moon, you reckless marvel.
In this floating black sphere, there are no edges,
just transformations. The microwave looks
kindly in the candle's amber
light. The curtains are full of possibilities.
Miraculous, this gift: how
nothing can reach you here. Not what you haven't done, not tomorrow's
OBGYN appointment, not all the wildfires and floods and hurricanes
piling up like megaphoned
questions you can't answer. The night
roils around you, only it's not the night, it's
something bigger, something that holds you, something
that tells you, gently but firmly, this can't last,
under no circumstances will this last.
Vellum moon, solicitous microwave—nothing
will stay. You've drawn
Xs through your obligations,
you're pleading for more time, but the power blares back,
zealous in its quest to return what you dropped. Here: every stone. Every needle.

WHY I RESPECT THE DOG

The dog weighs twelve pounds
and uses them as she pleases.
The king-size bed is not big enough.
Sleep-enabler, stretch-monger,
when she wants to be touched,
she offers up the narrow white arc
of her belly. When a loud face
crowds her, she growls. Or, depending
on the weather, the time, the face,
she doesn't. The dog knows
the precise creak of the cheese drawer
and waits. She is never wrong.
The dog does not care for rain.
The dog does not fret about the carpets.
The dog is on the table again,
and the sandwich crusts are gone,
the cereal milk is gone,
the cracker crumbs are gone.
She knows *down* but will not heed it.
Sometimes at night I leave her
sleeping on the couch, her eyes
flickering with dreams. From bed,
I hear her nails clicking down
the hall, fast, faster. She noses open
the door and launches herself
against me, her twelve pounds,
her punk-black fur. She wants
to be close, right now,
and so she is.

SUBURBAN BEAST

You live by the woods. The sunroom
looks out onto white oak, hackberry, pitch pine.

In high wind the limbs sing, and you
sing something else, a house song, song

of shelter and *mine*. You sing it until
you forget the trees. You never forget the trees.

Still, you sing. Brown leaves blanket your yard
and you make a show of your hackles rising.

How dare the leaves collect in gusted heaps
against the fence? You snarl and blow, set

to work again; pull, lug, mend. The truth is,
you love the crunching whispers

of the leaves. You could curl in them and sleep.
You could doze for days, sun-warmed.

You want the deer mice to nest in the crawlspace.
The ants that slip under the floorboards

and into the sunroom—what are they hurting,
with their invisible feet and silence?

But what kind of beast would you be
if you didn't drive them out? If you didn't

hoist the clawed rake, barb the foundation holes
with steel wool? This is your territory now.

You've claimed it. You'll bare your teeth to keep it.

NATURAL STATE

playground, after school

The children have shaken off
the shackles of calm.
The boy with the fragile arm
throws himself to the ground,
stands up, moshes into another boy
who throws him to the ground again.
A girl holds her side
as she runs, saying *ow ow ow ow*,
but does not stop running.
Another girl, passing her
without breaking stride,
advises, *Scream if you want.*
A boy dashes from one side
of the fenced perimeter to the other
and back, again and again,
yelling *beignet!* so loud
his voice is streaked and cracked.
He yells it over and over.
He is full of a thrill so vast
that the only way to keep existing
is to set it free.

MORTALITY

In the photos, the Italian ice cream cakes
are an impossibility of skill—the sheen

of black currant icing like a just-Zambonied
skating rink, the intricately labial lemon,

the sugar-string sculpture that defies physics
and the unspoken laws of what-is-necessary.

These frills and coils, these dried violets,
candied cherries, plum macarons as adornment—

the cakes are indecent, surely,
in their insistence on themselves,

in their insistence that you gaze at them
and then, having fallen impossibly,

irrevocably in love, open your mouth
and taste their disappearance.

That someone took the time to craft
such exquisite frivolity rankles, doesn't it?

Imagine if you spent your time
glazing mint leaves, shaving dark chocolate

into translucent ribbons. Imagine
if you spent your hours—your life—

the years of your hands' deftness—
making something so indulgent, so temporary,

something that ignites astonishment
and gladness so fleetingly, so flashingly,

and then, as everyone asks for more,
is gone.

IN THE WOODS ALL ANIMALS ARE LARGE

The difference between
a cougar stalking a deer
through gold leaves
and a squirrel dashing
over the underbrush
is no difference at all,
not when you're listening
from your backyard
to the woods' sudden
rustling. The robin
is the fox is the buck
is the bear, one beast
of wings and claws
and antlers. Your mind
is the same kind
of chimera, wearing
stroke, death, rupture,
breathing fire.
It's exhausting, isn't it,
the catastrophizing,
the endless possibilities?
A relief, then, to sit
in your backyard and listen
to the crackling leaves.
You have no control
over an animal that lives
outside your head.
What's coming for you
could be anything.

"THE DOOMSDAY CLOCK" SOUNDS LIKE THE TITLE OF A B-MOVIE

Some of us play villains: you can tell
by our eyebrows and schemes. Some of us
play scientists: you can tell by our elaborate
charts. Our sons and daughters play
neighborhood kids who ride bikes and yell
Hey mister! There are no other roles.
Near the end, the ticks pick up speed,
metronoming catastrophe. Headlines—
FIRE! FLOOD! CITY GONE!—
spin out of the black while violins swell,
staccato and frantic. We follow
the script. Plot and cajole. Sometimes
we imagine an audience filling the dark
theater. They boo and cheer in all
the right places as if, from our bright
burning screen, we can hear them.

ON THE HOTTEST DAY OF THE SUMMER I WATCH A HERON FLY OVERHEAD

The heat is a slow, inevitable weight,
thick like lava slurping over dark ash.
In the yard my kids are arguing
and I'm vaguely angry,
a low-level friction somewhere
at the nexus of my boys' shouting
and the earth's rapid burning
and the sweat pooling
at the small of my back.

When the heron cuts across
the blue sky, I stop. Watch it
until it passes beyond the tall trees.
My first thought, once it's gone,
is of this poem. *Flight* something,
smallness something, *perspective,*
cooling, in spite of.

But to melt the heron
into metaphor is a violence.
It's not a salve or symbol.
Not harbinger or amulet.
It will not save us.

What I know:
I saw it. It's still here.
So, for now, are we.

PAPER WASP (AN APOLOGY)

The day before we sprayed
your just-begun nest,
we watched through the window
as you worried woodpulp
and saliva into hexagons.
I had not seen before
your precise, elegant eyes
from an inch away,
or your fleet legs' urgency
as they built. We inched
our big faces closer,
safe on the other side
of the glass, yes, but our children
play in the yard.
You of all creatures
should understand.
You who with lancet and toxin
protect what you've built.
You who lunge
to meet threat with threat.
You should know
how swiftly violence
can bloom from fear.

This is what I told myself
as I watched you
making something
in the fierce July sun,
the entire yard bright
with your potential doom.
The finches in the maple.
The red plastic bat.
The hammock that doubles
as jungle gym.
The mantis.
The magpie.
And I'm sorry that we ended
your elegant eyes,
your tenacity. I'm sorry
that our fear was stronger
than your work.

DEAR DOGWOOD

Dear dogwood, what the hell?
Why all the blooming, raucous and bright,
like there isn't an apocalypse at your feet?
The toxic sprays. The runoff. The dryer lint
caught in the drainage grate. See, the bike rack
gets it, all stolid in gunmetal and rust.
The lamppost, grim, unbending. But
look at the daffodils—Jesus! The dandelion
poking its grinning sunhead through the mulch
that someone spread so carefully just
last week. All you organic fools, flowering
despite it all. The Ford Explorer,
ruining the earth every day, is festooned
with your wet pink blossoms like
a poacher wearing a necklace of teeth,
and still you keep dropping more
and more every time the wind gusts.
Squirrels spiral up and down your trunk.
Everywhere: chittering robins, nattering jays.
Why all these festivities? How? *Oh killjoy*,
I imagine you saying, your soft petals
on my neck like a cocktail-cool hand,
even disaster is a party if you dress for it.

THE CURATOR OF THE EARTH MUSEUM SPEAKS OF PEOPLE

We know that the people loved beautiful things.
From their earliest kind they were fools for shine
and order: necklaces strung with tiny seashells,
amulets of amethyst and chalcedony. The people
loved tall buildings with many glinting windows;
from these they would survey the land below them,
parceled into fields or city blocks. In their later iterations,
they crafted vehicles that required the earth's blood
to run, but this they extracted in quiet violences
in remote places, and then it was as if their shining
transports ran on nothing. The people lit their homes
with delicate glass globes, filaments vibrating
with a white-hot glow. Sometimes this glow came
from the earth's bones, which the people mined
at great cost. Sometimes it came from scientists,
who learned that atoms could be harnessed to fuel both
light and ruin. The power plants where the atoms fizzed
were ugly concrete things, but the people built them far
from their most beautiful places and were content.

When the earth began dying, the people would not
believe it; this we know from our archival work.
There was too much beauty to be had, they thought,
too many emeralds and ostriches and villas.
The people had not made flying machines and elegant
spoons and great glass observation decks just to stay home
and worry. And so they did not worry, because
they loved beauty so much. The people were governed

by beauty, driven by it as their cattle were driven
by dogs. They could not see beyond it. Our archivists
are still cataloguing the data the people ignored;
the people had evolved to shutter themselves
from anything unbeautiful. In this their cleverness
warred against their nature: they devised ways to save
themselves, then rejected them again and again.
The wind turbines would interrupt the infinite blue
horizon, solar panels would pox the verdant fields,
and this was too great a cost for people who loved
beauty above all else. Also, they did not like to think
of death. And so they went on with their amulets
and filaments, their observation decks and quiet violences.
They would be pleased to know that, though the organic
earth was of course unsalvageable, our digs have yielded
exquisite relics: silver stovetops, banisters, millions
of clear plastic vessels. Here in the museum, we honor
the people's devotion to beauty: out of respect,
before we display their bones or baubles,
we take care to polish them to gleaming.

THE HOWWOLF

It sleeps next to you, rises
when you rise. Presses close
in the kitchen, the cemetery,
the subway. It matches
its gait perfectly to your own.
In its soft mouth it carries
whatever you need. Open your hand
and it's yours: how to remember
that everything ends while still practicing times tables
and keeping the baseboards dust-free.
How to bathe a dog.
A baby.
A rigid-with-rage toddler.
How to say *child, we've done it, we've wrecked the earth*
already, before you even arrived, and
how to say *look at that heron, look, there he goes,*
you can hear his wings, how amazing is that!
Open your hand and it's yours:
how to remove a splinter.
A tick.
A stray hair.
How to apply winged eyeliner.
How to select a ripe cantaloupe.
How to teach your mind every afternoon
when you hear screams from the school behind your house
to think *playground, tag*.
How to sharpen a pencil evenly.
Fold a t-shirt.
Press a four-leaf clover.

How to sit at night on a child's bedroom floor on request,
flickering with how everything ends.
How not to let the dark room be lit by your flickering.
How to wait, and wait, and then, when the child is asleep,
how to slip out quietly, the beast beside you, into
the living room that blazes with everything,
absolutely everything you've ever learned.

QUAIL

As in to cower, to hunch down
in fear. As in the bird

I couldn't identify in Sedona
all those years back when I was

worried and sad about the things
I hadn't yet done and how terrible

they might turn out when I did them.
In the desert, I saw the bird's

odd little ornamentation,
its cartoon-quick speed, and tried

to make its strangeness distraction
or balm. It didn't work.

In the birds' peck-and-dash
I saw my own frantic vigilance.

I was scared I'd stay scared,
scared I'd make myself small

and root always in the soft dirt
at my feet. Later, back home,

I researched, learned that quail
can fly when necessary but prefer land.

That, running, they're agile and swift,
skilled at escaping. All my equations—

I = small bird; small bird = fear;
fear = frozen in place—were wrong.

I've always been bad at math
and soothsaying. I didn't hide

in those red rocks forever.
I didn't go small. I went home.

I stayed scared but not still.
I never turned bird. Only

more human.

JUST BECAUSE THE EARTH IS DYING DOESN'T MEAN I'VE STOPPED WANTING THINGS

I want aspen, of course.
I want honeybees divebombing my beer.
I want heavy, draping snow
and ice-cased oaks.

I want made things, too:
red glass planter, opal cocktail
ring, sequined slippers that flip
from silver to teal.

I get the irony: I'll be gone
before they are.

Still.

There are so many ornately-carved doors
on this planet, and I want to walk
through all of them.

The prediction for tomorrow
is tornadoes, straight-line winds.
Tonight we have plans for tacos.
Later, board games.

The world will not end in fire,
though there will be some of those.

I haven't told my sons yet
about the koalas.

I want every art museum, in every city:
the cool marble floors, the soporific lighting.
I want centuries of impossible
accomplishment.

The world will not end in ice.
That, at this point, seems pretty clear.

I am grateful for every good breath.
I am grateful for the good way I stretched
this morning, my body starfished

to each corner of the bed.

I want more stretching.

I want more starfish.

A recent study found
that deep-sea starfish have been
eating microplastics for decades,
nylon and polyester threading
their dime-sized stomachs.

I want every shade of yellow: ochre, mustard, dandelion, canary.

I want more movies with anachronistic dancing.

I want gin infused with desert plants.

I want gin and dancing and all the yellows forever.

Maybe not forever. Not really. But forever
is how my wanting feels,
that deep down.
If you pitched a penny down its darkness,
you would never hear it land.

The world may end in water.
Already cities are disappearing.

Before the virus, my husband and I
planned a trip to Italy.
In our research, we Googled
Venice airport and *floods*.
Everything had reopened.
We build back and back and back.
Now on the airport's website,
parking lot swab tests
and suspended flights.

More likely the world will end
haphazard—some flooding
& crumbling, some flames
in green places, the unloved creatures

gone first and then the soft ones.

Contaminant masks.

Late night TV jokes
about hazmat suits.

Once, we took the kids to New York.
When the downpour started, we bought umbrellas
from a bodega, but it was too late
for my marigold flats. I'd bought them
because they were sustainable,
washable, and because I loved their ethical
brightness. Still, a flood's a flood.
The water was up to our ankles.
Later, in our rented walk-up,
we laughed, got the kids into warm,
dry pjs. We were fine, which was
all that mattered. The next day
we'd wake up early
to see the bones of extinct
and marvelous monsters.

VIDEO: MURMURATION, GLASGOW

The second thing that astonishes you is the people
who don't look up. A teenager hunches
over his phone, the birds at his back.
A woman brisk-walks. A guy in khakis
looks studiously away, as if stopping to marvel
might unman him. What, you wonder,
is wrong with them? In the sky
a black whirlwind is morphing
into mushroom cloud, genitals, tornado,
eels in love. Soot dance. Opposite of snow.
You refresh the video again and again
the way one might worry a scab.
When the ache begins, it's subtle at first.
You can't quite parse it, this wanting
something you can never have even as
you're having it. But soon it's almost unbearable,
isn't it, the undulation, the impossible
sift-and-shadow of the starlings?
You're watching the miracle again and again
but you're not bird or shadowsift,
and you can't hold the fluttering in your hands
or on your tongue. You'll never enter
this vastness, not really. You stand up.
Reheat your coffee. Get back to work.
If you could find that man, that woman
on her quick way elsewhere—
you'd walk with them, wouldn't you?
You'd go with them into the night,
unmoored now and sadder, but open forever.

"PAINTMAKERS ARE RUNNING OUT OF THE COLOR BLUE"

—news headline

Which feels right. Blue has always been
too easy to come by. And yellow.
And crimson. And silver, god, silver.
Children, for Christmas this year
I've procured for you a swatch
of blue cotton. Husband, happy
anniversary, here is an unobstructed view
of a cerulean billboard. Let it be enough
just to say it. Let me love what I have
while I have it. The factories are still
churning out blue doors and skateboards
and lamps. My oldest son's bedroom is blue.
My nails. Our Honda. Dear husband,
dear children, dear parents, dear sister,
dear nephews, dear friends who
send postcards and mix Manhattans
and ask after dogs, I love you, right now
I love you. On the floor at my feet
is the box from my new bike helmet.
It's azure, the bright creamy shade
of a just-mixed vat. I see it. I let it stun me.

FLAMINGO IN ASSATEAGUE BEACH

"While there is no definite explanation for the flamingo's unexpected arrival, Assateague Park staff tells WBOC that recent hurricanes and storms may have disrupted its migration path."

For a flash of a second, a hot pink bolt,
I love the headline: the flame insinuated,
the imperative, the mild transgression,
then the sleek seams of *teague* and *beach*,
and quicker than clop or caw I'm inside

a dream, and a flamboyance of absurd birds
populates the shore where wild ponies
still roam, and Assateague is vaster with *yes*
than any unreal planet, and soon the polar bears
settle there, the pangolin, the harp seal,

soon glasswing butterflies and orchid mantis
dot the beachgrass, soon crimson sunbirds
and kestrels perch side by side, not because
the tides have waylaid them, not because
migration paths became wind tunnels,

not because spring starts in winter or
winter never comes, but because
some great thoughtful eye decided this island
off the coast of Virginia was the proper locus
for color and clamor, Assateague as oasis

of the impossible, its sand-barred marshes
feathered forever the color of sunrise,
the winds so calm that, no matter where
you are, you can hear the soft velvet
exhalations of animals fearless and home.

THIS IS HOW WE KEEP GOING

By the surf, a mussel shell
wedged into wet sand, edge-up.
Someone could cut their foot on that,
I thought, and turned it flat,
while behind me the entire beach
rippled with mussel shells.

THOMPSON ISLAND TRAIL, IN FALL

Deer crackle and flit into the pathless woods,
where our sons want to explore,
where the sign says *don't.* The marsh
is flooded today as we cross the footbridge.
No, not flooded—full. We can hardly see
the mussels under the rushing water,
but we know they're there. We walk through
the giant hardwood forest, the stands
of loblolly pine. The fallen oak, rotted and rich
with lichen and turkeytail mushrooms.
At the trail's end overlook, the fiddler crabs,
impossibly invented creatures, scuttle
and glitter blackly in the marsh mud,
their unwieldy single claws upraised.
Yes, you can go off trail, we tell our sons.
We watch the crabs, the marshgrass, the abandoned
red rowboat. Our dog pulls to keep going.
Behind us, the boys are climbing a tree,
their voices sharp as they bicker. The sky
blares blue. An egret stalks invisible fish,
strikes at the water like a snake, swallows,
stalks again. The silence between us
hums with bay-spark and late October.
Impossibly invented, all of it.

ACKNOWLEDGMENTS

I'm grateful to the editors of the following publications where these poems first appeared, sometimes in different form.

32 Poems: "Probably It Will be Summer Again"
A Public Space: "Break"
About Place Journal: "This Is How We Keep Going"
AGNI: "Poem Not Intended to Stand in Contrast to Anything for Once"
American Poetry Review: "At 42, I Consider Becoming a Zookeeper," "The Curator of the Earth Museum Speaks of People"
Blackbird: "'The Doomsday Clock' Sounds Like the Title of a B-Movie," "Some Things Are Not Hypothetical," "The Whywolf"
Cherry Tree: "Shooting Gallery, or What I Don't Say When I Write to My Senators Again About Gun Safety"
Cincinnati Review: "Sand Crab (An Admission)"
Cortland Review: "Paintmakers Are Running Out of the Color Blue"
Court Green: "Dear Dogwood"
diode: "On the Hottest Day of the Summer, I Watch a Heron Fly Overhead," "Poem Begun While Watching My Son's Gymnastics Class"
EcoTheo Review: "Engine, or What I Am Learning from the Animals"
Florida Review: "Flamingo in Assateague Bay," "The Wherewolf"
Ilanot Review: "My Father Takes Me to See the 32-Foot-Tall Stainless Steel Madonna Sculpture in Downtown Wilmington DE"
Los Angeles Review: "Bullet Is a Good Name for a Horse," "Thompson Island Trail, in Fall"
Love's Executive Order: "Oh, Today Was Actually the Longest Day of the Year"
Missouri Review: "The Horse Girls"
On the Seawall: "What Do You Make of That?"
Poetry: "In the Woods All Animals Are Large"

Poetry Northwest: "Just Because the Earth Is Dying Doesn't Mean I've Stopped Wanting Things"
SIERRA: "Earth, Sometimes I Try to Play It Casual"
Southern Indiana Review: "The Whenwolf"
The Southern Review: "Abecedarian for the Power Outage," "If/When"
The Sun: "Why I Respect the Dog"
Tupelo Quarterly: "Burrowing Crayfish (An Ode)"
Water~Stone Review: "I Wonder if the Guy Who Cat-Called Me in the Blockbuster Parking Lot When I Was 15 Ever Thinks About That"
Waxwing: "I've Known You All My Life," "The Howwolf," "The Whowolf"
West Branch: "Mortality," "Urgency"
wildness: "What I Want to Believe About the Vireos"

Thank you to my parents, Debbie and Carl, and my sister, Sarah, for their endless and unflagging love and support. I love you and am so lucky to have you—and to always have had you—in my corner. Thank you to Ron, Julie, Trevor, and everyone else in the ever-widening circle of family I love so well, and thank you to your own circles for welcoming me in.

Thank you to the friends and colleagues with whom I've had countless invaluable conversations about writing, art, kids, dogs, Skee-Ball, and lots of other things, in particular Nicky Beer, Brian Barker, Amy Wilkinson, Nathan Oates, Emily Spivack, Ian Chillag, Becky Hagenston, Troy DeRego, Saddiq Dzukogi, Rich Lyons, Megan Bean, and Ben Harvey.

Special thanks to Maggie Smith for her unerring eye and her friendship.

Thank you to my Mississippi State colleagues, friends, and students.

Thank you to the Mississippi Arts Commission for a grant that helped to support the writing of this book.

Thank you to Nickole Brown and January Gill O'Neil for their generosity and the gift of their poems.

Enormous thanks to everyone at Saturnalia Books, including Henry Israeli, Timothy Liu, Rebecca Lauren, and Sarah Wetzel, as well as to artist Robin Vuchnich for this book's cover.

Thank you to Sam and Wyatt, for being the greatest kids / humans / co-adventurers I could ever imagine. And thank you to Mike, for everything. Mike, I'm so glad I met you at the beginning of this century. You can stiff me five bucks any time.

BIO

Catherine Pierce is the author of the poetry collections *Danger Days, The Tornado Is the World, The Girls of Peculiar,* and *Famous Last Words,* as well as the memoir *Foxes for Everybody.* Her work has appeared in *The Best American Poetry, The New York Times, The Nation, American Poetry Review,* and elsewhere, and has won two Pushcart Prizes. A recipient of fellowships from the National Endowment for the Arts and the Academy of American Poets, she served as Poet Laureate of Mississippi from 2021 to 2025.

Also by Catherine Pierce

Danger Days

The Tornado Is the World

The Girls of Peculiar

Famous Last Words

Foxes for Everybody

Dear Beast was printed in Adobe Caslon
www.saturnaliabooks.org

DEAR BEAST

CATHERINE PIERCE

saturnalia | BOOKS

Distributed by Independent Publishers Group
Chicago

Saturnalia Books
2816 North Kent Rd.
Broomall, PA 19008
info@saturnaliabooks.com

ISBN: 978-1-947817-92-0 (print), 78-1-947817-93-7 (ebook)
Library of Congress Control Number: 2025947313

Book and Cover design by Robin Vuchnich

Distributed by:
Independent Publishing Group
814 N. Franklin St.
Chicago, IL 60610
800-888-4741